2019-2020

Girl Scouts Planner

Troop No :

Table Of Contents

r

Leader

Name :	Cell No :	Background Checked : Y / N
Address :		
Email Address :		
Notes :		

Co Leaders and Volunteers

Name :	Cell No :	Background Checked : Y / N
Address :		
Email Address :		
Notes :		

Name :	Cell No :	Background Checked : Y / N
Address :		
Email Address :		
Notes :		

Name :	Cell No :	Background Checked : Y / N
Address :		
Email Address :		
Notes :		

Name :	Cell No :	Background Checked : Y / N
Address :		
Email Address :		
Notes :		

Name :	Cell No :	Background Checked : Y / N
Address :		
Email Address :		
Notes :		

Co Leaders and Volunteers

Name :	Cell No :	Background Checked : Y / N
Address :		
Email Address :		
Notes :		

Name :	Cell No :	Background Checked : Y / N
Address :		
Email Address :		
Notes :		

Name :	Cell No :	Background Checked : Y / N
Address :		
Email Address :		
Notes :		

Name :	Cell No :	Background Checked : Y / N
Address :		
Email Address :		
Notes :		

Name :	Cell No :	Background Checked : Y / N
Address :		
Email Address :		
Notes :		

Co Leaders and Volunteers

Name :	Cell No :	Background Checked : Y / N
Address :		
Email Address :		
Notes :		

Name :	Cell No :	Background Checked : Y / N
Address :		
Email Address :		
Notes :		

Name :	Cell No :	Background Checked : Y / N
Address :		
Email Address :		
Notes :		

Name :	Cell No :	Background Checked : Y / N
Address :		
Email Address :		
Notes :		

Name :	Cell No :	Background Checked : Y / N
Address :		
Email Address :		
Notes :		

TROOP ROSTER

Girl's Name :	Cell No :	School :
Parent's Name :	Cell No :	
Parent's Name :	Cell No :	
Address :	Email Address :	
Emergency Contact :	Cell No :	
Allergies :	Age :	Birthday :

Girl's Name :	Cell No :	School :
Parent's Name :	Cell No :	
Parent's Name :	Cell No :	
Address :	Email Address :	
Emergency Contact :	Cell No :	
Allergies :	Age :	Birthday :

Girl's Name :	Cell No :	School :
Parent's Name :	Cell No :	
Parent's Name :	Cell No :	
Address :	Email Address :	
Emergency Contact :	Cell No :	
Allergies :	Age :	Birthday :

Girl's Name :	Cell No :	School :
Parent's Name :	Cell No :	
Parent's Name :	Cell No :	
Address :	Email Address :	
Emergency Contact :	Cell No :	
Allergies :	Age :	Birthday :

TROOP ROSTER

Girl's Name :	Cell No :	School :
Parent's Name :	Cell No :	
Parent's Name :	Cell No :	
Address :	Email Address :	
Emergency Contact :	Cell No :	
Allergies :	Age :	Birthday :

Girl's Name :	Cell No :	School :
Parent's Name :	Cell No :	
Parent's Name :	Cell No :	
Address :	Email Address :	
Emergency Contact :	Cell No :	
Allergies :	Age :	Birthday :

Girl's Name :	Cell No :	School :
Parent's Name :	Cell No :	
Parent's Name :	Cell No :	
Address :	Email Address :	
Emergency Contact :	Cell No :	
Allergies :	Age :	Birthday :

Girl's Name :	Cell No :	School :
Parent's Name :	Cell No :	
Parent's Name :	Cell No :	
Address :	Email Address :	
Emergency Contact :	Cell No :	
Allergies :	Age :	Birthday :

TROOP ROSTER

Girl's Name :	Cell No :	School :
Parent's Name :	Cell No :	
Parent's Name :	Cell No :	
Address :	Email Address :	
Emergency Contact :	Cell No :	
Allergies :	Age :	Birthday :

Girl's Name :	Cell No :	School :
Parent's Name :	Cell No :	
Parent's Name :	Cell No :	
Address :	Email Address :	
Emergency Contact :	Cell No :	
Allergies :	Age :	Birthday :

Girl's Name :	Cell No :	School :
Parent's Name :	Cell No :	
Parent's Name :	Cell No :	
Address :	Email Address :	
Emergency Contact :	Cell No :	
Allergies :	Age :	Birthday :

Girl's Name :	Cell No :	School :
Parent's Name :	Cell No :	
Parent's Name :	Cell No :	
Address :	Email Address :	
Emergency Contact :	Cell No :	
Allergies :	Age :	Birthday :

TROOP ROSTER

Girl's Name :	Cell No :	School :
Parent's Name :	Cell No :	
Parent's Name :	Cell No :	
Address :	Email Address :	
Emergency Contact :	Cell No :	
Allergies :	Age :	Birthday :

Girl's Name :	Cell No :	School :
Parent's Name :	Cell No :	
Parent's Name :	Cell No :	
Address :	Email Address :	
Emergency Contact :	Cell No :	
Allergies :	Age :	Birthday :

Girl's Name :	Cell No :	School :
Parent's Name :	Cell No :	
Parent's Name :	Cell No :	
Address :	Email Address :	
Emergency Contact :	Cell No :	
Allergies :	Age :	Birthday :

Girl's Name :	Cell No :	School :
Parent's Name :	Cell No :	
Parent's Name :	Cell No :	
Address :	Email Address :	
Emergency Contact :	Cell No :	
Allergies :	Age :	Birthday :

Health Info

Girl's Name	Health Issues	Notes

Health Info

Girl's Name	Health Issues	Notes

Birthday Tracker

January	February	March

April	May	June

July	August	September

October	November	December

2019

JANUARY
M	T	W	T	F	S	S
	1	2	3	4	5	6
7	8	9	10	11	12	13
14	15	16	17	18	19	20
21	22	23	24	25	26	27
28	29	30	31			

FEBRUARY
M	T	W	T	F	S	S
				1	2	3
4	5	6	7	8	9	10
11	12	13	14	15	16	17
18	19	20	21	22	23	24
25	26	27	28			

MARCH
M	T	W	T	F	S	S
				1	2	3
4	5	6	7	8	9	10
11	12	13	14	15	16	17
18	19	20	21	22	23	24
25	26	27	28	29	30	31

APRIL
M	T	W	T	F	S	S
1	2	3	4	5	6	7
8	9	10	11	12	13	14
15	16	17	18	19	20	21
22	23	24	25	26	27	28
29	30					

MAY
M	T	W	T	F	S	S
		1	2	3	4	5
6	7	8	9	10	11	12
13	14	15	16	17	18	19
20	21	22	23	24	25	26
27	28	29	30	31		

JUNE
M	T	W	T	F	S	S
					1	2
3	4	5	6	7	8	9
10	11	12	13	14	15	16
17	18	19	20	21	22	23
24	25	26	27	28	29	30

JULY
M	T	W	T	F	S	S
1	2	3	4	5	6	7
8	9	10	11	12	13	14
15	16	17	18	19	20	21
22	23	24	25	26	27	28
29	30	31				

AUGUST
M	T	W	T	F	S	S
			1	2	3	4
5	6	7	8	9	10	11
12	13	14	15	16	17	18
19	20	21	22	23	24	25
26	27	28	29	30	31	

SEPTEMBER
M	T	W	T	F	S	S
						1
2	3	4	5	6	7	8
9	10	11	12	13	14	15
16	17	18	19	20	21	22
23	24	25	26	27	28	29
30						

OCTOBER
M	T	W	T	F	S	S
1	2	3	4	5	6	
7	8	9	10	11	12	13
14	15	16	17	18	19	20
21	22	23	24	25	26	27
28	29	30	31			

NOVEMBER
M	T	W	T	F	S	S
			1	2	3	
4	5	6	7	8	9	10
11	12	13	14	15	16	17
18	19	20	21	22	23	24
25	26	27	28	29	30	

DECEMBER
M	T	W	T	F	S	S
						1
2	3	4	5	6	7	8
9	10	11	12	13	14	15
16	17	18	19	20	21	22
23	24	25	26	27	28	29
30	31					

2020

JANUARY
M	T	W	T	F	S	S
	1	2	3	4	5	
6	7	8	9	10	11	12
13	14	15	16	17	18	19
20	21	22	23	24	25	26
27	28	29	30	31		

FEBRUARY
M	T	W	T	F	S	S
					1	2
3	4	5	6	7	8	9
10	11	12	13	14	15	16
17	18	19	20	21	22	23
24	25	26	27	28	29	

MARCH
M	T	W	T	F	S	S
						1
2	3	4	5	6	7	8
9	10	11	12	13	14	15
16	17	18	19	20	21	22
23	24	25	26	27	28	29
30	31					

APRIL
M	T	W	T	F	S	S
		1	2	3	4	5
6	7	8	9	10	11	12
13	14	15	16	17	18	19
20	21	22	23	24	25	26
27	28	29	30			

MAY
M	T	W	T	F	S	S
				1	2	3
4	5	6	7	8	9	10
11	12	13	14	15	16	17
18	19	20	21	22	23	24
25	26	27	28	29	30	31

JUNE
M	T	W	T	F	S	S
1	2	3	4	5	6	7
8	9	10	11	12	13	14
15	16	17	18	19	20	21
22	23	24	25	26	27	28
29	30					

JULY
M	T	W	T	F	S	S
		1	2	3	4	5
6	7	8	9	10	11	12
13	14	15	16	17	18	19
20	21	22	23	24	25	26
27	28	29	30	31		

AUGUST
M	T	W	T	F	S	S
					1	2
3	4	5	6	7	8	9
10	11	12	13	14	15	16
17	18	19	20	21	22	23
24	25	26	27	28	29	30
31						

SEPTEMBER
M	T	W	T	F	S	S
	1	2	3	4	5	6
7	8	9	10	11	12	13
14	15	16	17	18	19	20
21	22	23	24	25	26	27
28	29	30				

OCTOBER
M	T	W	T	F	S	S
			1	2	3	4
5	6	7	8	9	10	11
12	13	14	15	16	17	18
19	20	21	22	23	24	25
26	27	28	29	30	31	

NOVEMBER
M	T	W	T	F	S	S
						1
2	3	4	5	6	7	8
9	10	11	12	13	14	15
16	17	18	19	20	21	22
23	24	25	26	27	28	29
30						

DECEMBER
M	T	W	T	F	S	S
	1	2	3	4	5	6
7	8	9	10	11	12	13
14	15	16	17	18	19	20
21	22	23	24	25	26	27
28	29	30	31			

AUGUST 2019

Mon	Tue	Wed	Thu	Fri	Sat	Sun
29	30	31	1	2	3	4
5	6	7	8	9	10	11
12	13	14	15	16	17	18
19	20	21	22	23	24	25
26	27	28	29	30	31	1

SEPTEMBER 2019

Mon	Tue	Wed	Thu	Fri	Sat	Sun
26	27	28	29	30	31	1
2	3	4	5	6	7	8
9	10	11	12	13	14	15
16	17	18	19	20	21	22
23 / 30	24	25	26	27	28	29

OCTOBER 2019

Mon	Tue	Wed	Thu	Fri	Sat	Sun
30	1	2	3	4	5	6
7	8	9	10	11	12	13
14	15	16	17	18	19	20
21	22	23	24	25	26	27
28	29	30	31	1	2	3

NOVEMBER 2019

Mon	Tue	Wed	Thu	Fri	Sat	Sun
28	29	30	31	1	2	3
4	5	6	7	8	9	10
11	12	13	14	15	16	17
18	19	20	21	22	23	24
25	26	27	28	29	30	

DECEMBER 2019

Mon	Tue	Wed	Thu	Fri	Sat	Sun
25	26	27	28	29	30	1
2	3	4	5	6	7	8
9	10	11	12	13	14	15
16	17	18	19	20	21	22
23 / 30	24 / 31	25	26	27	28	29

JANUARY 2020

Mon	Tue	Wed	Thu	Fri	Sat	Sun
30	31	1	2	3	4	5
6	7	8	9	10	11	12
13	14	15	16	17	18	19
20	21	22	23	24	25	26
27	28	29	30	31		

FEBRUARY 2020

Mon	Tue	Wed	Thu	Fri	Sat	Sun
27	28	29	30	31	1	2
3	4	5	6	7	8	9
10	11	12	13	14	15	16
17	18	19	20	21	22	23
24	25	26	27	28	29	1

MARCH 2020

Mon	Tue	Wed	Thu	Fri	Sat	Sun
24	25	26	27	28	29	1
2	3	4	5	6	7	8
9	10	11	12	13	14	15
16	17	18	19	20	21	22
23 / 30	24 / 31	25	26	27	28	29

APRIL 2020

Mon	Tue	Wed	Thu	Fri	Sat	Sun
30	31	1	2	3	4	5
6	7	8	9	10	11	12
13	14	15	16	17	18	19
20	21	22	23	24	25	26
27	28	29	30	1	2	3

MAY 2020

Mon	Tue	Wed	Thu	Fri	Sat	Sun
27	28	29	30	1	2	3
4	5	6	7	8	9	10
11	12	13	14	15	16	17
18	19	20	21	22	23	24
25	26	27	28	29	30	31

JUNE 2020

Mon	Tue	Wed	Thu	Fri	Sat	Sun
1	2	3	4	5	6	7
8	9	10	11	12	13	14
15	16	17	18	19	20	21
22	23	24	25	26	27	28
29	30	1	2	3	4	5

JULY 2020

Mon	Tue	Wed	Thu	Fri	Sat	Sun
29	30	1	2	3	4	5
6	7	8	9	10	11	12
13	14	15	16	17	18	19
20	21	22	23	24	25	26
27	28	29	30	31		

AUGUST 2020

Mon	Tue	Wed	Thu	Fri	Sat	Sun
27	28	29	30	31	1	2
3	4	5	6	7	8	9
10	11	12	13	14	15	16
17	18	19	20	21	22	23
24 / 31	25	26	27	28	29	30

Attendance Tracker

Date	Meeting / Event	Girls' Names																	

Attendance Tracker

Date	Meeting / Event	Girls' Names																	

Attendance Tracker

Date	Meeting / Event	Girls' Names														

Snack Signup Sheet

Meeting Date	Girl's Name	Notes

Snack Signup Sheet

Meeting Date	Girl's Name	Notes

Meeting / Event Planner

Date and Place of Meeting / Event :

Pre-Meeting Preparation :

Opening Ceremony :

Activities :

Supplies If Any Needed :

Cleanup and Closing :

Notes :

Meeting / Event Planner

Date and Place of Meeting / Event :

Pre-Meeting Preparation :

Opening Ceremony :

Activities :

Supplies If Any Needed :

Cleanup and Closing :

Notes :

Meeting / Event Planner

Date and Place of Meeting / Event :

Pre-Meeting Preparation :

Opening Ceremony :

Activities :

Supplies If Any Needed :

Cleanup and Closing :

Notes :

Meeting / Event Planner

Date and Place of Meeting / Event :

Pre-Meeting Preparation :

Opening Ceremony :

Activities :

Supplies If Any Needed :

Cleanup and Closing :

Notes :

Meeting / Event Planner

Date and Place of Meeting / Event :

Pre-Meeting Preparation :

Opening Ceremony :

Activities :

Supplies If Any Needed :

Cleanup and Closing :

Notes :

Meeting / Event Planner

Date and Place of Meeting / Event :

Pre-Meeting Preparation :

Opening Ceremony :

Activities :

Supplies If Any Needed :

Cleanup and Closing :

Notes :

Meeting / Event Planner

Date and Place of Meeting / Event :

Pre-Meeting Preparation :

Opening Ceremony :

Activities :

Supplies If Any Needed :

Cleanup and Closing :

Notes :

Meeting / Event Planner

Date and Place of Meeting / Event :

Pre-Meeting Preparation :

Opening Ceremony :

Activities :

Supplies If Any Needed :

Cleanup and Closing :

Notes :

Meeting / Event Planner

Date and Place of Meeting / Event :

Pre-Meeting Preparation :

Opening Ceremony :

Activities :

Supplies If Any Needed :

Cleanup and Closing :

Notes :

Meeting / Event Planner

Date and Place of Meeting / Event :

Pre-Meeting Preparation :

Opening Ceremony :

Activities :

Supplies If Any Needed :

Cleanup and Closing :

Notes :

Meeting / Event Planner

Date and Place of Meeting / Event :

Pre-Meeting Preparation :

Opening Ceremony :

Activities :

Supplies If Any Needed :

Cleanup and Closing :

Notes :

Meeting / Event Planner

Date and Place of Meeting / Event :

Pre-Meeting Preparation :

Opening Ceremony :

Activities :

Supplies If Any Needed :

Cleanup and Closing :

Notes :

Meeting / Event Planner

Date and Place of Meeting / Event :

Pre-Meeting Preparation :

Opening Ceremony :

Activities :

Supplies If Any Needed :

Cleanup and Closing :

Notes :

Meeting / Event Planner

Date and Place of Meeting / Event :

Pre-Meeting Preparation :

Opening Ceremony :

Activities :

Supplies If Any Needed :

Cleanup and Closing :

Notes :

Meeting / Event Planner

Date and Place of Meeting / Event :

Pre-Meeting Preparation :

Opening Ceremony :

Activities :

Supplies If Any Needed :

Cleanup and Closing :

Notes :

Meeting / Event Planner

Date and Place of Meeting / Event :

Pre-Meeting Preparation :

Opening Ceremony :

Activities :

Supplies If Any Needed :

Cleanup and Closing :

Notes :

Meeting / Event Planner

Date and Place of Meeting / Event :

Pre-Meeting Preparation :

Opening Ceremony :

Activities :

Supplies If Any Needed :

Cleanup and Closing :

Notes :

Meeting / Event Planner

Date and Place of Meeting / Event :

Pre-Meeting Preparation :

Opening Ceremony :

Activities :

Supplies If Any Needed :

Cleanup and Closing :

Notes :

Meeting / Event Planner

Date and Place of Meeting / Event :

Pre-Meeting Preparation :

Opening Ceremony :

Activities :

Supplies If Any Needed :

Cleanup and Closing :

Notes :

Meeting / Event Planner

Date and Place of Meeting / Event :

Pre-Meeting Preparation :

Opening Ceremony :

Activities :

Supplies If Any Needed :

Cleanup and Closing :

Notes :

Meeting / Event Planner

Date and Place of Meeting / Event :

Pre-Meeting Preparation :

Opening Ceremony :

Activities :

Supplies If Any Needed :

Cleanup and Closing :

Notes :

Meeting / Event Planner

Date and Place of Meeting / Event :

Pre-Meeting Preparation :

Opening Ceremony :

Activities :

Supplies If Any Needed :

Cleanup and Closing :

Notes :

Meeting / Event Planner

Date and Place of Meeting / Event :

Pre-Meeting Preparation :

Opening Ceremony :

Activities :

Supplies If Any Needed :

Cleanup and Closing :

Notes :

Meeting / Event Planner

Date and Place of Meeting / Event :

Pre-Meeting Preparation :

Opening Ceremony :

Activities :

Supplies If Any Needed :

Cleanup and Closing :

Notes :

Meeting / Event Planner

Date and Place of Meeting / Event :

Pre-Meeting Preparation :

Opening Ceremony :

Activities :

Supplies If Any Needed :

Cleanup and Closing :

Notes :

Meeting / Event Planner

Date and Place of Meeting / Event :

Pre-Meeting Preparation :

Opening Ceremony :

Activities :

Supplies If Any Needed :

Cleanup and Closing :

Notes :

Meeting / Event Planner

Date and Place of Meeting / Event :

Pre-Meeting Preparation :

Opening Ceremony :

Activities :

Supplies If Any Needed :

Cleanup and Closing :

Notes :

Meeting / Event Planner

Date and Place of Meeting / Event :

Pre-Meeting Preparation :

Opening Ceremony :

Activities :

Supplies If Any Needed :

Cleanup and Closing :

Notes :

Meeting / Event Planner

Date and Place of Meeting / Event :

Pre-Meeting Preparation :

Opening Ceremony :

Activities :

Supplies If Any Needed :

Cleanup and Closing :

Notes :

Meeting / Event Planner

Date and Place of Meeting / Event :

Pre-Meeting Preparation :

Opening Ceremony :

Activities :

Supplies If Any Needed :

Cleanup and Closing :

Notes :

Meeting / Event Planner

Date and Place of Meeting / Event :

Pre-Meeting Preparation :

Opening Ceremony :

Activities :

Supplies If Any Needed :

Cleanup and Closing :

Notes :

Meeting / Event Planner

Date and Place of Meeting / Event :

Pre-Meeting Preparation :

Opening Ceremony :

Activities :

Supplies If Any Needed :

Cleanup and Closing :

Notes :

Meeting / Event Planner

Date and Place of Meeting / Event :

Pre-Meeting Preparation :

Opening Ceremony :

Activities :

Supplies If Any Needed :

Cleanup and Closing :

Notes :

Meeting / Event Planner

Date and Place of Meeting / Event :

Pre-Meeting Preparation :

Opening Ceremony :

Activities :

Supplies If Any Needed :

Cleanup and Closing :

Notes :

Meeting / Event Planner

Date and Place of Meeting / Event :

Pre-Meeting Preparation :

Opening Ceremony :

Activities :

Supplies If Any Needed :

Cleanup and Closing :

Notes :

Meeting / Event Planner

Date and Place of Meeting / Event :

Pre-Meeting Preparation :

Opening Ceremony :

Activities :

Supplies If Any Needed :

Cleanup and Closing :

Notes :

Meeting / Event Planner

Date and Place of Meeting / Event :

Pre-Meeting Preparation :

Opening Ceremony :

Activities :

Supplies If Any Needed :

Cleanup and Closing :

Notes :

Meeting / Event Planner

Date and Place of Meeting / Event :

Pre-Meeting Preparation :

Opening Ceremony :

Activities :

Supplies If Any Needed :

Cleanup and Closing :

Notes :

Meeting / Event Planner

Date and Place of Meeting / Event :

Pre-Meeting Preparation :

Opening Ceremony :

Activities :

Supplies If Any Needed :

Cleanup and Closing :

Notes :

Meeting / Event Planner

Date and Place of Meeting / Event :

Pre-Meeting Preparation :

Opening Ceremony :

Activities :

Supplies If Any Needed :

Cleanup and Closing :

Notes :

Badge and Patch Tracker

Date	Badges and Patch Description	Girls' Names																

Badge and Patch Tracker

Date	Badges and Patch Description	Girls' Names																

Forms and Paperwork Tracker

Date	Forms or Paperwork To Be Done	Girls' Names																		

Forms and Paperwork Tracker

Date	Forms or Paperwork To Be Done	Girls' Names																		

Volunteer Signup Sheet

Event Date	Description of Event	Volunteers

Volunteer Signup Sheet

Event Date	Description of Event	Volunteers

Volunteer Signup Sheet

Event Date	Description of Event	Volunteers

Volunteer Signup Sheet

Event Date	Description of Event	Volunteers

Troop Dues and Fees Tracker

Date	Description (Membership Dues, Uniform, Field Trip Fees etc.,)	Girls' Names (Mark When Paid)														

Troop Dues and Fees Tracker

Date	Description (Membership Dues, Uniform, Field Trip Fees etc.,)	Girls' Names (Mark When Paid)																		

Troop Dues and Fees Tracker

Date	Description (Membership Dues, Uniform, Field Trip Fees etc.,)	Girls' Names (Mark When Paid)																	

Troop Dues and Fees Tracker

Date	Description (Membership Dues, Uniform, Field Trip Fees etc.,)	Girls' Names (Mark When Paid)																

Financial Ledger

Date	Description	Income $	Expense $	Balance $

Financial Ledger

Date	Description	Income $	Expense $	Balance $

Financial Ledger

Date	Description	Income $	Expense $	Balance $

Financial Ledger

Date	Description	Income $	Expense $	Balance $

Checking Account Tracker

Bank Name :	Address :
Phone Number :	Hours of Operation :
Account Number :	Routing Number :

Date	Transaction	Withdrawal	Deposit	Balance

Checking Account Tracker

Date	Transaction	Withdrawal	Deposit	Balance

Checking Account Tracker

Date	Transaction	Withdrawal	Deposit	Balance

Checking Account Tracker

Date	Transaction	Withdrawal	Deposit	Balance

Individual Girls' Product Sales Tracker

Date	Product	Girls' Names																	

Individual Girls' Product Sales Tracker

Date	Product	Girls' Names																		

Individual Girls' Product Sales Tracker

Date	Product	Girls' Names

Individual Girls' Product Sales Tracker

Date	Product	Girls' Names																

Individual Girls' Product Sales Tracker

Date	Product	Girls' Names																			

Individual Girls' Product Sales Tracker

Date	Product	Girls' Names																		

Cookie Booth Sales Tracker

Booth Location :   **Date :**

Cookie Name								
Price Per Box								
No of Boxes at the Start								
No of Boxes at the End								
Total No of Boxes Sold								
Total $ Earned								

Girl Scout's Name	Starting Time	End Time	No of hours	No of Boxes Sold

Total No of Boxes Sold :	**Starting Cash Amount :**
	Ending Cash Amount :
$$ in Donations :	**Credit Card Sales :**
Total Booth Sales Profit :	

Cookie Booth Sales Tracker

Booth Location :   **Date :**

Cookie Name							
Price Per Box							
No of Boxes at the Start							
No of Boxes at the End							
Total No of Boxes Sold							

Total $ Earned							

Girl Scout's Name	Starting Time	End Time	No of hours	No of Boxes Sold

Total No of Boxes Sold :	**Starting Cash Amount :**
	Ending Cash Amount :
$$ in Donations :	**Credit Card Sales :**
Total Booth Sales Profit :	

Cookie Booth Sales Tracker

Booth Location :   **Date :**

Cookie Name							
Price Per Box							
No of Boxes at the Start							
No of Boxes at the End							
Total No of Boxes Sold							

Total $ Earned							

Girl Scout's Name	Starting Time	End Time	No of hours	No of Boxes Sold

Total No of Boxes Sold :	**Starting Cash Amount :**
	Ending Cash Amount :
$$ in Donations :	**Credit Card Sales :**
Total Booth Sales Profit :	

Cookie Booth Sales Tracker

Booth Location :   **Date :**

Cookie Name								
Price Per Box								
No of Boxes at the Start								
No of Boxes at the End								
Total No of Boxes Sold								

Total $ Earned								

Girl Scout's Name	Starting Time	End Time	No of hours	No of Boxes Sold

Total No of Boxes Sold :	**Starting Cash Amount :**
	Ending Cash Amount :
$$ in Donations :	**Credit Card Sales :**

Total Booth Sales Profit :

Cookie Booth Sales Tracker

Booth Location :   **Date :**

Cookie Name								
Price Per Box								
No of Boxes at the Start								
No of Boxes at the End								
Total No of Boxes Sold								
Total $ Earned								

Girl Scout's Name	Starting Time	End Time	No of hours	No of Boxes Sold

Total No of Boxes Sold :	**Starting Cash Amount :**
	Ending Cash Amount :
$$ in Donations :	**Credit Card Sales :**
Total Booth Sales Profit :	

Cookie Booth Sales Tracker

Booth Location :   **Date :**

Cookie Name							
Price Per Box							
No of Boxes at the Start							
No of Boxes at the End							
Total No of Boxes Sold							
Total $ Earned							

Girl Scout's Name	Starting Time	End Time	No of hours	No of Boxes Sold

Total No of Boxes Sold :	**Starting Cash Amount :**
	Ending Cash Amount :
$$ in Donations :	**Credit Card Sales :**
Total Booth Sales Profit :	

Cookie Booth Sales Tracker

Booth Location :   **Date :**

Cookie Name								
Price Per Box								
No of Boxes at the Start								
No of Boxes at the End								
Total No of Boxes Sold								
Total $ Earned								

Girl Scout's Name	Starting Time	End Time	No of hours	No of Boxes Sold

Total No of Boxes Sold :	**Starting Cash Amount :**
	Ending Cash Amount :
$$ in Donations :	**Credit Card Sales :**
Total Booth Sales Profit :	

Cookie Booth Sales Tracker

Booth Location :   **Date :**

Cookie Name								
Price Per Box								
No of Boxes at the Start								
No of Boxes at the End								
Total No of Boxes Sold								

Total $ Earned								

Girl Scout's Name	Starting Time	End Time	No of hours	No of Boxes Sold

Total No of Boxes Sold :	Starting Cash Amount :
	Ending Cash Amount :
$$ in Donations :	Credit Card Sales :

Total Booth Sales Profit :

Cookie Booth Sales Tracker

Booth Location :   **Date :**

Cookie Name								
Price Per Box								
No of Boxes at the Start								
No of Boxes at the End								
Total No of Boxes Sold								
Total $ Earned								

Girl Scout's Name	Starting Time	End Time	No of hours	No of Boxes Sold

Total No of Boxes Sold :	**Starting Cash Amount :**
	Ending Cash Amount :
$$ in Donations :	**Credit Card Sales :**
Total Booth Sales Profit :	

Cookie Booth Sales Tracker

Booth Location :   **Date :**

Cookie Name							
Price Per Box							
No of Boxes at the Start							
No of Boxes at the End							
Total No of Boxes Sold							

Total $ Earned							

Girl Scout's Name	Starting Time	End Time	No of hours	No of Boxes Sold

Total No of Boxes Sold :	**Starting Cash Amount :**
	Ending Cash Amount :
$$ in Donations :	**Credit Card Sales :**
Total Booth Sales Profit :	

Cookie Booth Sales Tracker

Booth Location :　　　　　　　　　　　　　　**Date :**

Cookie Name								
Price Per Box								
No of Boxes at the Start								
No of Boxes at the End								
Total No of Boxes Sold								
Total $ Earned								

Girl Scout's Name	Starting Time	End Time	No of hours	No of Boxes Sold

Total No of Boxes Sold :	**Starting Cash Amount :**
	Ending Cash Amount :
$$ in Donations :	**Credit Card Sales :**

Total Booth Sales Profit :

Cookie Booth Sales Tracker

Booth Location :   **Date :**

Cookie Name							
Price Per Box							
No of Boxes at the Start							
No of Boxes at the End							
Total No of Boxes Sold							

Total $ Earned							

Girl Scout's Name	Starting Time	End Time	No of hours	No of Boxes Sold

Total No of Boxes Sold :	Starting Cash Amount :
	Ending Cash Amount :
$$ in Donations :	Credit Card Sales :

Total Booth Sales Profit :

Notes and To-Do List

Notes	Date :

Notes	Date :

Notes and To-Do List

Notes	Date :

Notes	Date :

Notes and To-Do List

Notes	Date :

Notes	Date :

Notes and To-Do List

Notes	Date :

Notes	Date :

Notes and To-Do List

Notes	Date :

Notes	Date :

Notes and To-Do List

Notes	Date :

☐
☐
☐
☐
☐
☐
☐
☐
☐
☐
☐

Notes	Date :

☐
☐
☐
☐
☐
☐
☐
☐
☐
☐
☐

Notes and To-Do List

Notes	Date :

Notes and To-Do List

Notes	Date :

Notes	Date :

Notes and To-Do List

Notes	Date :

Notes	Date :

Notes and To-Do List

Notes	Date :

Notes	Date :

Notes and To-Do List

Notes	Date :

Notes	Date :

Notes and To-Do List

Notes	Date :

Notes	Date :

Notes and To-Do List

Notes | **Date :**

Notes | **Date :**

Notes and To-Do List

Notes	Date :

Notes	Date :

Notes and To-Do List

Notes	Date :

Notes	Date :

Notes and To-Do List

Notes | **Date :**

Notes | **Date :**

Notes and To-Do List

Notes | **Date :**

☐
☐
☐
☐
☐
☐
☐
☐
☐
☐
☐

Notes | **Date :**

☐
☐
☐
☐
☐
☐
☐
☐
☐
☐
☐

Notes and To-Do List

Notes	Date :

☐
☐
☐
☐
☐
☐
☐
☐
☐
☐
☐

Notes	Date :

☐
☐
☐
☐
☐
☐
☐
☐
☐
☐
☐

Notes and To-Do List

Notes	Date :

☐

☐

☐

☐

☐

☐

☐

☐

☐

☐

☐

Notes	Date :

☐

☐

☐

☐

☐

☐

☐

☐

☐

☐

☐

Notes and To-Do List

Notes	Date :

☐
☐
☐
☐
☐
☐
☐
☐
☐
☐
☐

Notes	Date :

☐
☐
☐
☐
☐
☐
☐
☐
☐
☐
☐

57262139R00086

Made in the USA
Middletown, DE
28 July 2019